ALL ABOUT

The Everglades

Karuna Eberl

BLUE RIVER PRESS

Indianapolis, Indi

T0182747

Published by Blue River Press
Indianapolis, Indiana
www.brpressbooks.com

Distributed by Cardinal Publishers Group
A Tom Doherty Company, Inc.
www.cardinalpub.com

ISBN: 978-1-68157-122-5

Cover Design: Tessa Schmitt
Book Design: Rick Korab
Cover Artist: Robert Perrish
Editor: Tessa Schmitt
Illustrator: Stefanie Geyer

Printed in the United States of America

10 9 8 7 6 5 4 3 2 1   30 31 32 23 24 25 26 27 28 29

Special thanks to The Friends of the Everglades for reading
All About the Everglades and helping our team produce the
most up-to-date and accurate book possible.

CONTENTS

ALL ABOUT

The Everglades

Grassy Waters: Meet the Everglades

At first glance, the Everglades look like a vast plain of grass. A carpet of tall, wispy blades stretches as far as the eye can see. At sunrise, the grasses appear bright orange. By lunchtime, they are green with freckles of brown. After a rain, when drops of water cling to the leaves, they look like glittering fields of diamonds.

Everglades National Park is one of the largest wetlands in the world, but the Everglades' ecological borders extend far beyond the park's boundaries.

"Pa-hay-Okee" is what Native Americans have called this land. That means "grassy waters."

Though the land might be covered with grass, this is no ordinary meadow. All through the grass flows a giant, slow-moving river. Its water invites animals of all sorts. Birds wade. Some of them have legs so long they are almost as tall as people. Frogs sing atop lily pads, chanting, "Brrr-eep. Brrr-eep." Alligators also prowl here, their eyes and tips of their noses barely peeking above the waterline.

Other animals in this marshy wilderness are less daunting. Otters prance along river banks. Flocks of ibis — social birds with spindly legs and long, curved beaks — poke for crabs in the mud. Around them, butterflies, almost lighter than air itself, float from flower to flower.

Here and there, islands of trees rise above the grass. Inside, some forests are swampy, dark, and mysterious, where moss dangles from trees and wild orchids grow. Others are tropical, where bright green leaves grow thick, shading lizards and panthers.

Where the grass ends, pine forests begin. Red-bellied woodpeckers patrol the skinny tree trunks.

Below, white-tailed deer and black bears wander. To the south, where the slow-moving water finally finds the ocean, manatees and dolphins swim between tangled mangrove islands.

Sometimes the Everglades are a land of extremes. Hurricanes roar. Sunshine blazes. Thunder crashes. Rain pours. Grass fires burn. All of these change the land. Most rejuvenate it, each in their own way.

The Everglades are one of the largest and most diverse wetlands in the world. Hundreds of bird species depend on it for nesting, resting, and refueling on their migrations. The Everglades also help people in many ways, providing clean air, water, and jobs.

People have a long history here. Native Americans, Spanish conquistadors, pioneers, settlers, farmers, real estate developers, and nature conservationists have all shaped it and left their mark. Today, the lush wilderness surrounding the Everglades still provides a home to the Seminole and Miccosukee people.

For all of its grandness, only half of the original Greater Everglades ecosystem still exists today. Of that, one fifth is protected within Everglades National Park. Each year, more than a million tourists visit the park. Exploring always brings surprises, like spotting a pink-colored roseate spoonbill, or finding colorful tree snails. Adventures are everywhere, too, from hiking through the forests to boating across the water.

Even though so many people love the Everglades, the grassy waters are in danger. Dams, pollution, human sprawl, invasive species, and climate change all threaten this delicate ecosystem. Today, people of all ages are working to save these wild lands. Preserving the Everglades ensures a safe home for plants, animals, and future generations of humans.

Everglades National Park was formally recognized on December 6, 1947 by President Harry S. Truman. The land, waters, and their biodiversity were then officially protected from human development.

CHAPTER ONE

Tiny Creatures, Giant Beasts

GEOLOGY & THE EVERGLADES THROUGH TIME

Throughout most of the last 180 million years, oceans covered what would become the Everglades. Sea stars with wispy limbs crawled the ocean floor. Above them swam torpedo-shaped squid and long-necked fish.

Some animals, like tarpon, looked almost like they do today. Others evolved into creatures like megalodons. These prehistoric sharks were longer than a school bus, with teeth the size of grapefruits. Stories about these giants usually steal the spotlight, but it was the smallest animals that changed everything.

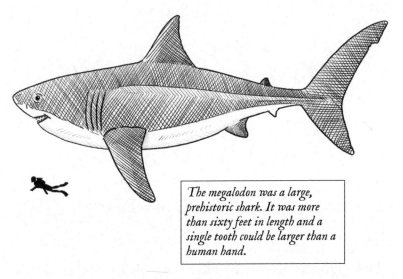

The megalodon was a large, prehistoric shark. It was more than sixty feet in length and a single tooth could be larger than a human hand.

Millions of generations of oysters, sea snails, and other tiny, even microscopic creatures lived in these waters. When they died, their shells and bones piled up on the ocean floor as sediment. Eventually the sediment turned into limestone rock, which remains underneath the Everglades today.

When ice ages came, huge amounts of water fell as snow in the northern part of the continent, forming glaciers. That caused sea level to fall and — ta da! — Florida become dry land. Eventually, the air warmed again. The ice melted and the water flowed into the oceans. This freezing and thawing of ice, and therefore the fall and rise of oceans, happened several times. Each time Florida went underwater, more tiny ocean creatures lived and died, resulting in growing amounts of limestone. But in some places the rock did not form from animals. Rather, the minerals that make up limestone, called calcium carbonate, solidified directly from the water.

The top layers of limestone that we find under most of the Everglades today began forming about 125,000 years ago. In contrast to the underlying limestone bedrock, this limestone formed when the ocean was shallow enough for tides and waves to move sediment particles back and forth. As this happened, calcium carbonate precipitated from the water and slowly formed little spheres called ooids.

Currents pushed the ooids into a ridge. On the east side, more ooids formed. On the back side, where the water was protected and calm, lived colonies of bryophytes (also called zooids). They were little mossy animals resembling coral. In time, the ooids and zooids became the rock layer named the Miami limestone.

Mega Land Creatures

When the most recent Ice Age made dry land in Florida, during the Pleistocene Epoch, land animals moved in. Some of the first settlers were mammoths. These curious, strong travelers made an epic journey that took many generations, from Asia, across an Arctic land bridge to North America. Then they traveled south through Central and South America. Over time, changing climate drove them north again to Florida, where it was warm and full of plants to feed their enormous appetites.

Southern Florida must have felt like paradise, but it was not yet the Everglades. The mammoths' trumpets did not echo across a marsh, but rather across woods and grasslands. The environment was probably much like the savanna of Africa today. And the mammoths were not alone.

Early horses, deer, and herds of camels grazed next to mini rhinos. Here lived huge beavers, tortoises, and armadillos the size of cars. Sloths that were bigger than elephants ate leaves from tree branches. Lions, wolves, and saber-toothed

Like elephants, Columbian mammoths didn't have much fur and they probably lived in herds.

cats stalked them all, in search of a meaty meal.

The scene must have been fantastic, containing more exotic wildlife than the plains of Africa today. But near the end of the last Ice Age, ten thousand years ago, most of the animals mysteriously died off. Only their bones and teeth remained. Today, scientists study those remains to try to figure out why the animals became extinct. Perhaps it was humans or maybe a changing climate.

Making the Everglades

The weather changed around the time of the last mammoths. Southern Florida became wet and subtropical. Rains became more frequent and heavier. The landscape transformed again. The Everglades would soon come to exist through a series of exceptional events.

Limestone bedrock is very porous, and it dissolves in acid. Rain and decaying plants both contain small amounts of acid. So as rain increased and more plants grew, acid formed many holes in the rock. Over time, dead plants decayed into a thick soil called peat. Peat is spongy and holds an

The Everglades landscape came to be through a process called weathering. Rainstorms, flooding, and other environmental processes can cause the land to change.

exceptional amount of water. The more holes that formed in the rock, the more places there were to hold water and peat.

Peat kept piling up. It grew particularly high in the middle of Florida, until a wall of peat dammed the water flowing south. The water collected into an enormous lake, today called Lake Okeechobee, the largest freshwater lake in Florida.

When the wet seasons came, water overflowed the peat dams of Okeechobee and flooded the land to the south. With regular floods, lots of rain, warm temperatures, plenty of peat, and all of those holes in the limestone, there was finally enough water to make the Everglades.

For five thousand years the Everglades stayed pretty much the same. It wasn't until about a century ago that it began to change, when people started building dams and canals to try to prevent floods and dry out the land for houses and farming. That made the Everglades smaller and created other problems, which you can learn more about in chapter six.

Despite these troubles, much of the marsh remains untamed and wild — and the Everglades endures as one of the most interesting places on Earth.

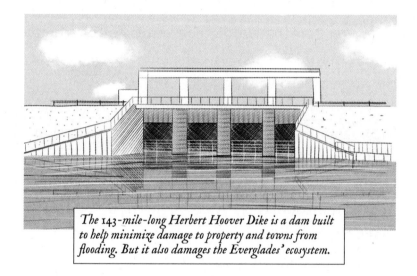

The 143-mile-long Herbert Hoover Dike is a dam built to help minimize damage to property and towns from flooding. But it also damages the Everglades' ecosystem.

Finding Limestone

Sometimes it's hard to see limestone in Everglades National Park because most of it is covered with plants, water, and peat. But here and there, you can see rocky patches poking out, which give a glimpse into ancient history.

Limestone in the park is usually light gray. It's lumpy and full of indentations. It looks a little bit like the surface of the moon. Scientists call that look "karst." Karst landscapes often also contain caves and sinkholes. Other examples of karst are the Mammoth Caves in Kentucky and parts of the Ozark mountains in Arkansas and Missouri.

Limestone is a soft rock. It's easy to scratch with a knife. If you see a rock you think is limestone, you can check to find out by pouring vinegar on it. If it fizzes, it's limestone! The reason it fizzes is because vinegar is an acid. It dissolves the calcium carbonate, the material from which limestone is made. That releases carbon dioxide, a gas, which rises to the surface of the rock in bubbles.

CHAPTER TWO

Tangled Roots to Lofty Pines

ECOSYSTEMS & HABITATS: A HOME FOR ALL

From Lake Okeechobee south to the Florida Bay, the Florida peninsula slopes ever so slightly downhill. Since the change in elevation is so gradual, water doesn't form traditional rivers. Instead, it travels as a broad, flat sheet across many miles, creating one of the world's largest wetlands.

The wetlands meander through fields of tall sawgrass, which grow atop spongy peat. Below that black muck, within the porous limestone bedrock, lies the Biscayne Aquifer. The Everglades recharge this natural storage tank, which provides drinking water for many millions of people who live and vacation in southern Florida.

Since life in the Everglades revolves around water, rain plays a pivotal role in the lives of its animals and plants. Here, there are just two seasons: dry and wet. Summers are hot and humid. Eighty percent of the year's rain (nearly five feet) falls during summer months, while winters (December through April) are dry and mild.

The Everglades are home to countless plants, including the butterfly orchid, which is found in trees.

An unusual diversity of life thrives in this subtropical climate. Around a thousand plant species grow here. They have adapted to survive the dramatic changes in water levels. Many of these plants can also grow on limestone, even though it offers few nutrients.

Animal species are plentiful as well; thousands of species of insects, hundreds of birds and fish, and dozens of reptiles, mammals, and amphibians call the Everglades home. The many animal and plant species have also adapted to living in wet and dry cycles. Many also live in very specific habitats.

The most obvious habitat in the Everglades is the sawgrass marsh, which covers much of the national park. The second-largest is the marine and estuary undersea saltwater world of Florida Bay. Elsewhere, four kinds of forests grow: hardwood hammocks, cypress domes, mangrove swamps, and pine rocklands. Lastly, there are freshwater sloughs, plus a number of other habitats and

The Everglades is special because of its diversity of landscapes and animals. Each habitat plays a role in the overall ecosystem.

Pond & Slough   Wet Prairie   Sawgrass Marsh   Freshwater Swamp   Hardwood Hammocks transitions zones, like wet prairies, freshwater marl prairies, coastal lowlands and freshwater swamps. Some animals spend time in several habitats, but many live only in the one that suits them best.

Sawgrass Marsh

Tall, skinny sawgrass is full of surprises, but the biggest is that it is sharp. The edge of each blade is full of tiny teeth. It's also not really a grass, but

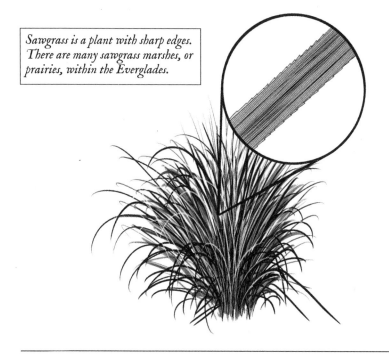

Sawgrass is a plant with sharp edges. There are many sawgrass marshes, or prairies, within the Everglades.

rather belongs to a family of plants called sedges. In the summer, the sawgrass grows through a sheet of water that might be waist high, but in the winter the ground is often dry enough to walk across.

The Everglades are often referred to as a swamp, but most of it is actually a marsh. Areas containing grass, sedges, and reeds are called marshes, whereas those with trees and shrubs are termed swamps.

Around the sawgrass, at the water's surface, live squishy, greenish blobs. These periphyton (pronounced pair-ee-fi-ton) are colonies of organisms, made mostly of bacteria and green algae. These lumps are some of the most important forms of life here. They don't look like much, but billions of years ago their ancestors began turning carbon dioxide into oxygen by photosynthesis. Because of them, air is breathable for all animals on Earth.

Today, periphyton are a vital part of the Everglades' circle of life. Bugs, snails, and other creatures eat the periphyton. Fish and birds eat the bugs. Turtles, birds, and alligators eat the fish. And lucky people get to watch it all happen.

Whatever the season, it's possible to hike

through, or rather above, some parts of the marsh on elevated boardwalk trails. Stand quietly for a little bit, and you will start to notice movement. A water strider skims along the surface. A spider mends her web. An egret lands. And a flock of wood storks soar overhead.

The Hardwood Hammocks

Here and there, hills rise from the marsh. Actually though, they aren't hills; they are forest hardwood hammocks with trees towering above the grass. Here the ground does not flood because it is a foot or two higher than the sawgrass marsh. Dry land allows tropical trees to grow, and trees make hammocks a comfortable place to escape from the hot sun.

Many small creatures who live in the hammocks never realize the world beyond their forest. They may spend their whole lives on a single, isolated tree island. Their island also protects them from fires because acid from decaying leaves dissolves the limestone surrounding their forest. Water then

An Inconvenient Tree

Poisonwood trees grow in the hammocks and other places in the Everglades, including along roadsides. Their black sap gives humans a painful rash. Be careful not to touch them or to stand under them in the rain. It's fun to appreciate them from afar though. Their berries are a favorite meal for rare white-crowned pigeons and other birds.

fills the holes, forming a ring — like a moat around a castle. When grass fires burn, they usually can't cross the moat to hurt the hammock.

While exploring a hammock, look for colorful liguus tree snails on branches. They are hard to spot at first, but worth the effort. Do not touch them; they are endangered. Collectors used to steal these beautiful snails from the forests, taking so many that some colors and patterns are now extinct.

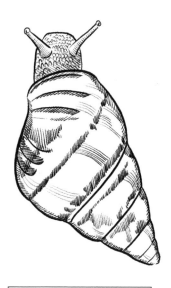

Other creatures often spotted in hammocks are butterflies, tree frogs, and lizards. The native green anole lizard turns from bright green to brown to hide itself.

Also look for strangler figs, with roots that hang down like thin vines, and gumbo limbo trees with red, peeling bark.

Liguus tree snails have developed more than fifty color patterns for their shells.

Cypress Domes

Looking out across the sawgrass, clusters of cypress trees also resemble islands, but they are the opposite of hammocks. These cypress domes grow in depressions, where the land is a little lower. Inside these forests lie primordial swamps that host a multitude of life.

Here, these water-loving cypress trees rise tall

Cypress trees grow in wetlands and help filter water. These slow-growing trees can live hundreds, if not thousands, of years.

and dark, blocking out most of the sun. Their tops might reach 125 feet, while woody extensions from their roots poke up out of the dark water. These exposed knobs are called "cypress knees." They look a little like stalagmites. Scientists believe these knees help the trees get oxygen and stabilize their lofty trunks, though that's just a theory, and the true reason remains a mystery waiting to be solved.

Epiphytes (aka air plants) are another set of peculiar plants found in cypress domes. They grow on other plants. Instead of penetrating the ground, their roots wrap around cypress branches and take in water and other nutrients from rain and dust in the air. Orchids and bromeliads are epiphytes that grow in the Everglades. Some of them are so rare that they exist nowhere else in Florida.

Cypress domes are also the domain of snakes and frogs. Some wading birds, like ibis and wood storks, like to nest here. The trees provide a protected place to raise their chicks. If you wish to explore these swamps, the easiest time to visit them is in the spring, when the ground is driest.

Visitors can follow park rangers through knee-deep waters to get up close and personal with the landscape of the Everglades.

Freshwater Sloughs

The deepest waters in the marshes and swamps are in sloughs (pronounced slews). In the dry season, animals who depend on the water gather in these boggy rivers, making them a great place to watch wildlife. Dragonflies dance along tops of plants. Red-winged blackbirds snap up meals of bugs. Herons stalk fish and frogs among the lily pads and reeds. And, of course, the alligators are always hanging out nearby.

Mangroves — Gateway to the Ocean

Eventually the Everglades' slow-moving waters reach the ocean. Here, on the border between the fresh and salt water, lies the tangled domain of mangroves. Their thick woodland of twisted branches makes the perfect home for many creatures. Nesting birds, small crabs, and lizards all hide here.

Underwater, mangroves make a nursery for tiny, vulnerable sea creatures. Baby sharks, snappers, barracudas, and countless other fish all grow up in the safety of messy mangrove roots until they are big enough to enter open water. So do horseshoe crabs, crocodiles, and turtles.

Mangrove forests also protect the land. Their sturdy roots and branches keep the shore from eroding during hurricanes and high tides. Mangroves are unusual trees, because they can live in salt water. They form a barrier that keeps salt from the land and filters nutrients and toxins from freshwater before it reaches the ocean.

Some mangrove islands have sandy beaches, where sandpipers skitter about eating shellfish. In the winter, bald eagles keep a keen eye out for their favorite meal: fish. But ospreys are the main birds of prey here. Look for their massive nests of woven sticks. Hungry chicks peek out above the walls and

The best time to bird watch is during the dry season (December through April). This is when birds are most concentrated around the water that remains, and when some migrating birds have settled in to stay warm.

squawk when they are hungry (which they almost always are). Mom and Dad take turns fishing all day.

Marine & Estuarine

Where mangroves give way to Florida Bay, a marine world begins. Close to shore, where rivers meet the bay, estuaries are formed. In this brackish habitat lives a rich diversity of species who have adapted to water that is less salty than the ocean, but saltier than an inland river.

Slightly farther out, beds of seagrass wave gently with the currents. Spiny lobsters and conchs travel the seafloor. Stingrays hunt crabs. Green sea turtles and gentle manatees graze on seagrass and the algae it holds.

Florida Bay stretches for 800 square miles, from the southern end of the Everglades to the islands of the Florida Keys. Out here, animals and plants are not always easy to distinguish from one another. Sponges, some of which look like giant cauldron pots anchored to the shallow seafloor, are actually animals who filter and clean the water. Corals are also animals, which grow in many shapes, from delicate fans to rocky lumps.

Sea cucumbers look like dark, spiny pickles. These relatives of starfish are the earthworms of the bay, breaking up organic matter and recycling it into nutrients for all. Upside-down jellyfish called Cassiopeia also look like plants. They are farmers, who wave their fluffy tentacles at the sun, so algae in their tissues can make food from photosynthesis.

The deepest depths of Florida Bay are only about nine feet, and most of it is less than three. That makes boating here tricky but rewarding. Some people enjoy fishing. Others simply like watching wildlife, since the shallow waters make it easy to spot sponges, rays, and dolphins from above.

Blacktip sharks are recognizable by the black spots on the edges of their fins, hence where they got their name. The species is "Near Threatened" due to overfishing and habitat destruction.

Pine Rocklands — a.k.a. Pinelands

While the bay holds the deepest depths, the pine rocklands make up the Everglades' highest points. Elevations here reach seven or eight feet above sea level. That might not seem very high, but "way up" there it almost never floods. The ground is hard and dry and home to a different set of plants and animals.

Forests of tall, thin pines shoot straight up. Below, many kinds of short palms cover the ground. Look for the saw palmetto with its scrubby, sharp leaves. Plants with fern-like leaves might be coontie, a type of cycad. A thousand years ago, Calusa people depended on coontie roots (also called arrowroot) for food, and a hundred years ago Seminoles used them to make a thick porridge called sofkee. Today people still eat sofkee, but they usually make it from cornmeal.

Many animals also find food in this forest. White-tailed deer graze the grasses and wildflowers. Black bears forage for fruit. At night, scorpions scuttle through the dirt and dead leaves eating bugs. Above, bats fly under the starlight, gobbling their fill of flying insects.

Pine rocklands once covered a lot of the Everglades, but now they are almost gone. Most of the trees were cut down to make room for Miami and other cities and suburbs. Where once there were forests, today there are parking lots, malls, houses, factories, and grocery stores. In fact, only two percent of pine rocklands remain, making them one of the most endangered habitats in the world. This makes a day spent hiking or bicycling through them particularly special.

Fire

Lightning sometimes starts fires in the sawgrass marshes, prairies, and pineland forests. Though destructive, natural wildfires are important for both habitats. In the sawgrass marshes, they burn back sedges and grasses, which helps water flow more freely. In the pinelands, fire clears away

Prescribed burns have long been used in the Everglades. They benefit vegetation and wildlife, since they mimic natural wildfires that help rejuvenate nature.

understory plants that might otherwise take over, which enables new trees to sprout and grow. In both places, fire is a healthy part of nature.

Florida is the most hurricane-prone state in the U.S. These natural disasters can have sustained wind speeds starting at 74 miles per hour, and the speeds can exceed 160 mph.

Hurricanes

Many powerful hurricanes have hit the Everglades. The winds are so strong that they can rip all the leaves off of the trees. After a hurricane, everything looks brown and dead. But native plants and animals have adapted in interesting ways to survive. It might take many months, but little by little, the plants turn green again and wildlife returns. Not everything survives every storm, though. Here and there are stands of dead, gray trees. They are ghostly, yet beautiful reminders of the power of nature.

CHAPTER THREE

Chirps, Grunts, and Growls

WILDLIFE IN THE EVERGLADES

If you are fortunate enough to be out walking in the Everglades, stop and listen for a moment. At first, all might sound quiet in the solitude of the wilderness. But soon, noises become apparent.

"Chee-ee-ee-ee-ee-ee." Crickets and cicadas are almost always going on about something.

"Woouu. Ou-oo-oo-oo-oo-uh." A barred owl calls out. "Wahh-ah-ah-ah-ah-ow." Her mate answers back.

Off in the distance an alligator rumbles out a low, bass-filled growl. "Uhhhrrrr. Grrrraah. Arruuhhh."

The Everglades are actually a noisy place. They are full of life. Each reptile, bird, mammal, fish,

See and hear animals as you ride through the Everglades! Tram tours allow visitors to see the Everglades in a short amount of time.

and insect tells a fascinating story. Unfortunately, all of these characters can't possibly fit into a single chapter, so below are just a few of the animals who call the Everglades home.

Reptiles

Lizards, snakes, and turtles prowl this wilderness, but alligators are the Everglades' most famous reptile residents. They can be spotted basking along trails and floating in ponds. As an apex predator, they have a big job. The health of the Everglades depends on them.

Like wolves in the tundra and sharks in the oceans, alligators keep plant and animal communities balanced. Alligators also dig holes in the cypress domes, which fill with water. As winter creeps in, and rivers and marshes dry up, the creatures who aren't able to trek to the safety of the deeper sloughs — like little fish, snails, and turtles — can survive in the holes until the rains return.

Crocodiles also live in the Everglades. They are rare and shy, so spotting one is special. Most people don't know it, but here's how to distinguish them from alligators. First of all, think about where

Alligator   *Crocodile*

You can tell alligators from crocodiles by their snout shapes, teeth, and habitats.

they are. Alligators like fresh water, but crocodiles prefer saltwater, so crocs usually hang out near the mangroves, closer to the ocean. Also, crocodile skin is grayish-green and they have more pointed, V-shaped snouts, versus alligators, which are almost black and have wider, U-shaped snouts. Plus, when crocs' mouths are closed, some of their bottom teeth still stick out, giving them a toothy grin.

Mammals

The two largest mammals that roam the Everglades (besides people) are Florida panthers and black bears. Panthers — also called mountain lions, pumas, or cougars, depending on what part of the country they're in — are endangered and secretive. Even people who live in the Everglades their whole lives may never see one. Most people never see black bears either, but sometimes you can tell if they've traveled nearby. Look for their scat (yes, that's poop) on the trail. It'll be a pile about the size of a shoe, with some seeds, berries, or maybe a little fur in it.

You might catch a glimpse of deer, raccoon, or opossum skittering across the trail. Opossums are a misunderstood bunch. Some people call them pests, but they are actually favorable neighbors. They eat rats and cockroaches and are immune to venomous snakes and rabies.

Gray foxes sometimes patrol the woods. One of their special skills is climbing trees (so long as the trees are leaning over a bit), which they do while hunting mice and birds. Flying squirrels also live among the pines. People sometimes mistake them for birds, since they can glide far enough to clear twenty cars in a single leap. Flying squirrels are nocturnal, so look for them in the moonlight.

Compared to the typical cottontail, marsh rabbits have thick, dense fur that makes them waterproof and comfortable in their soggy surroundings.

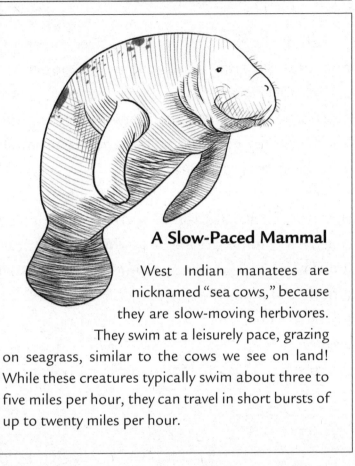

A Slow-Paced Mammal

West Indian manatees are nicknamed "sea cows," because they are slow-moving herbivores. They swim at a leisurely pace, grazing on seagrass, similar to the cows we see on land! While these creatures typically swim about three to five miles per hour, they can travel in short bursts of up to twenty miles per hour.

Skunks, river otters, Everglades mink, and bobcats make up a few of the other characters roaming the wilds. Though there are about forty different kinds of mammals here, they are seldom seen compared with other kinds of creatures — especially the ones with feathers.

Roseate spoonbills are easy to spot with their pink coloring. Young ones are lighter in color, then darken as they age.

Birds

There are almost as many species of birds in the Everglades as there are days in a year. They wade in the marsh, sing from the trees, soar through the skies, and float on the water. Each one comes with its own peculiar habits.

Brown pelicans nose-dive face-first into the ocean to scoop up fish. Anhingas and cormorants hold their breath and swim underwater to find a fishy meal. Reddish egrets twirl and leap like dancers during their hunt. And great blue herons are patient. They stand perfectly still waiting for the right snack to swim within reach. Great egrets look a lot like blue herons, except that they're white and slightly smaller.

Feathered Migrations

As the snow melts across the Great Plains and the northern forests, the spring migration begins. Birds who stayed warm through the winter in Central and South America start their journeys north. Many stop off in the Everglades to refuel. Red-tailed hawks feed on small birds and rodents while making their ways to places like Ohio, New York, and Canada. Warblers, vireos, and thrushes gobble up berries and insects before continuing on to destinations like Michigan and New Jersey. Then, when the snow clouds build again in the fall, they stop back on their way south.

Wood storks are white like great egrets, but taller and bulkier with black wingtips. To find fish, wood storks stick their bill underwater and shuffle their feet to scare up fish. Their pink toes also look like the worms fish like to eat. When a wood stork bill touches a fish, it snaps so quickly that scientists believe wood storks may have the fastest reflexes of any vertebrate (that's an animal with a backbone, like fish, birds, mammals, and reptiles).

Small birds also live in the Everglades. Some stay here year-round, like the Cape Sable seaside sparrow. Since they are the same color as the grass, they are hard to see. But their songs are easy to recognize. "Tweet, tweet, tweet, buzzzzz-zzzz-zzzz." Other fliers, like ruby-throated hummingbirds, live here only in winter. They travel as far as 2,000 miles from places including the mountains of Vermont and Maine, just to spend a few months in Florida's grassy marsh.

It's easy to appreciate the beauty of a tiny hummingbird, but what about a vulture? "Ew! Gross!" That's what some people say of vultures. But those people have never been lucky enough to meet one, so they don't realize the stereotype is undeserved. Intelligent and social, vultures are upstanding members of the community. They rarely kill other living things — animals or plants — to survive. Instead, they eat creatures who have already died. It might seem like a distasteful way to make a living, but we have them to thank for cleaning up the roadsides and keeping diseases from spreading.

In the Everglades, vultures have also developed a curious taste — windshield wipers. Once in a while, they like to pull them off of cars. So, keep an eye out when you park at a visitor center.

Amphibians

The Everglades are not entirely land, nor are they all water. They are something in between — which is just what amphibians need. Frogs and toads start their lives as tadpoles in the water. As they grow up, they lose their gills and breathe air. Like mammals, they breathe through their lungs. Unlike mammals, they can also breath through their skin.

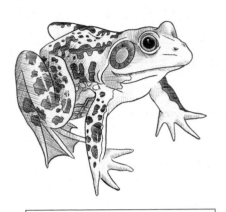

Each species of frog has its own sound. The pig frog (shown here) makes a pig-like snorting sound.

Some frogs are named for the noises they make, like the pig frog and cricket frog. Spend an evening outside, and it's likely you'll hear both sing their serenades. Pig frogs stay close to water, living in places such as ponds, sloughs, and sawgrass marshes. Others, like the common green treefrog and pinewoods treefrog, prefer to live in the branches. Pinewoods treefrogs are very rare and only ever grow as large as a chili bean, which makes them hard to see. But it's easy to know when they are around. Their call sounds like someone transmitting a message in Morse code.

All amphibians, and especially frogs, give scientists a good idea of whether or not an ecosystem is healthy, because they are sensitive to water levels and pollution. They might also tell us other things, like the weather forecast. Seminole folk stories teach children that the more the frogs are singing, the greater the chance it will soon rain.

Fish — and Crustaceans and Mollusks, too

Just as some amphibians are named after mammals, the Gulf toadfish got its name the other way around. They are one of the few fish that humans can hear. They whistle and grunt, and sometimes sound a little like a toad.

"Booo-boo. Booo-boo." The male calls out. If he makes his noise properly and loud enough, he might attract a female. If she meets him and is impressed, she will lay her eggs. But it's up to the male to stick around and guard them until they hatch.

Nearly as many kinds of fish live in the Everglades as birds. Some, like the toadfish, live among the sandy, seagrass, and shallow rocky bottoms of Florida Bay. Nurse sharks and stingrays (which are also types of fish) swim through here, searching for meals of animals who live in seashells (mollusks) and spiny lobsters (crustaceans). Other fish sometimes make appearances right below the docks, like barracuda, snapper, and tarpon.

Life is less predictable for the freshwater fish who live inland. With wet and dry seasons, they face extra challenges. As the rains stop, some make their way to the deeper sloughs. Others, like the bowfin, stay put. They can survive in water with very low oxygen levels, and even if their holes dry up, they aren't completely out of luck. When that happens, they burrow into the mud and aestivate (like hibernate) until the rains replenish their waterways.

Insects and Spiders

To insects in the Everglades, it must seem like everyone is out to get them. Birds, frogs, toads, lizards, snakes, fish, opossums, foxes, bears, and even other insects eat insects. Some, like mosquitoes, keep their species alive by breeding in large numbers. Others have developed more unusual solutions.

Bright orange-yellow Lubber grasshoppers — nicknamed Halloween grasshoppers — are so big

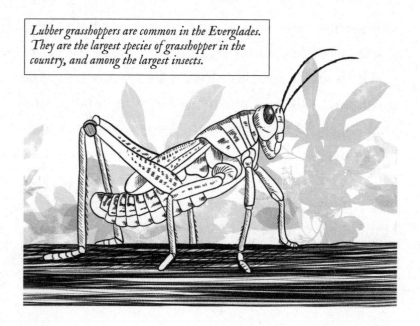

Lubber grasshoppers are common in the Everglades. They are the largest species of grasshopper in the country, and among the largest insects.

they barely fit in a person's hand. They are slow, but they have no need to run. They taste bad to anything that might eat them. If something picks them up, they also let out a foaming spray.

If a bug looks like a fire-fly in the Everglades, chances are it's a luminescent click beetle. At night it appears to have glowing green eyes, which are actually spots on its back end. It uses those, along with clicking and jumping, to confuse predators and attract mates.

Elsewhere, giant spiderwebs hang between trees. These often belong to golden orb weavers, which can grow five inches long including their bodies and legs. They are among the oldest kinds of spider, with ancestors dating back at least 165 million years.

There are more than 100 butterfly species within the Everglades, including Gulf fritillaries (shown here). If you see a brighter-colored fritillary flying around a duller-colored one, that could be a male courting a female.

Accidentally running into such a big arachnid can be startling, but their venom isn't dangerous to humans. Only two spiders in the Everglades can seriously hurt a person — black widows and brown recluses — both of which people rarely encounter.

Endangered Species

Sadly, many plants and animals in the Everglades are facing extinction. West Indian manatees, most species of sea turtles, Florida panthers, and wood

The Everglades is home to five sea turtle species. These endangered reptiles use Everglades National Park as a nesting area.

storks are some of the most famous. A few that don't get as much attention are Everglades snail kites, leafwing butterflies, Miami tiger beetles, Florida bonneted bats, and Key tree-cactus. Pollution from farms, factories, and houses; water flow disruption from dams and canals; loss of habitats from new neighborhoods; and climate change all contribute to their struggles. Another challenge is invasive species.

But there are some success stories as well. Thanks to conservation efforts, American crocodiles and American alligators are no longer endangered. They're great examples of how people can help rebound species' populations.

Invasive Species

Many plants and animals that are not native to southern Florida end up in the wild — sometimes because people don't know the disastrous consequences of freeing their unwanted pets. Because these exotic species have no natural predators, they take over ecosystems. Some of the most serious threats to the Everglades today are Burmese pythons, walking catfish, and many species of imported lizards. These non-native species quickly outcompete or even eat native wildlife.

Pythons are such a problem in the Everglades that they have eaten nearly all of the small mammals, including 98% of possums, 99% of raccoons and nearly 80% of marsh rabbits. They also eat a lot of native birds and reptiles. The loss of all of these native species is creating what biologists call a "trophic cascade," which means dramatic, negative changes to the ecosystem. We still don't know how the Everglades will ultimately change because of this imbalance.

Beyond the Everglades, pythons have recently started spreading to Key Largo in the Florida Keys, where they are causing problems, too, especially for endangered Key Largo woodrats.

CHAPTER FOUR

Shell Warriors & Conquistadors

EARLY EVERGLADES PEOPLES & THE EUROPEANS

People have lived in southern Florida for as long as the Everglades have existed. It's certainly possible they were here well before that — maybe even long enough to have walked with mammoths and saber-toothed cats. It's hard to know, because if there were villages at that time, most of the evidence would be underwater now. Back then, sea level was about three hundred feet lower than it is today because of the ice ages.

The Calusa People

The first southern Florida residents we do know a

bit about are the Calusa people and their neighbors: the Tequesta, Ais, Jenga, Mayaimi, and Jobe tribes. Their ancestors lived in southern Florida for at least 2,000 years. They handed down the skills, knowledge, and strength to thrive in harmony with such a challenging environment. Most of what we know about them, however, starts in the 1500s when Europeans first encountered them.

The Calusa (kah-LOO-sah) were the largest of the tribes, and their society held political influence over the others. Spanish accounts describe them as tall, powerful, elite warriors, who wore their hair long. The women dressed with skirts of Spanish moss, and the men donned breechcloths. Breechcloths are belts with a flap of woven palm or deerskin draped over the front to cover up. Both men and women adorned themselves with carved jewelry from shells and animal bones.

They built their villages atop mounds, which kept them safe from floods and tides. The largest towns had plazas for gathering, temples for worshiping, and houses that were big enough to sleep many people. Between the houses were complex systems of canals for transportation of people and goods. They devised ways to corral fish into holding pens, called water courts, to keep them alive until they needed food. Unlike most cultures this large, the Calusa did very little, if any, farming. Most of their food came from fishing, hunting, and gathering berries and roots.

One of the reasons the Calusa were able to build a complex society — one more like a kingdom than a tribe — was because they lived near marine estuaries, which are some of the most biodiverse (plant and animal filled) ecosystems on Earth. Unlike other hunter-gatherer communities who had to migrate when food was scarce, the Calusa always had plenty. (But later, when the Spanish came, many of them (the Spanish) starved because they didn't realize they could eat the sea life. Some even ate their horses to survive!)

Another way the Calusa had to be resourceful was with tools. South Florida doesn't have varied rocks like flint or chert from which to make tools like arrowheads and scrapers, so they used the resources they did have — shark teeth, shells, and

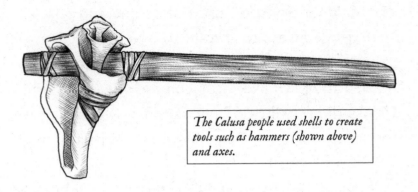

The Calusa people used shells to create tools such as hammers (shown above) and axes.

bones. The Calusa are sometimes called the "Shell Indians" because they depended on shells for everything from shovels and hammers to drinking cups and fishhooks. They also used them to hollow out logs for canoes.

Water, of course, was central to life in the Everglades and southern Florida, so the Calusa were skilled boaters. They traversed the marshes to hunt and visit other tribes. They probably even voyaged more than 90 miles across the treacherous Florida Strait to Cuba and further into the Caribbean to trade. It could have been on one of these visits that they first heard about the white-sailed ships headed their way.

Europeans Invade

Christopher Columbus was not the first European to reach the Americas. Viking Leif Erikson made it here almost 500 years earlier. But when Columbus landed in the Bahamas in 1492, he changed everything. His arrival set off a chain of events that devastated every culture in the Caribbean and the Americas.

Invading explorers seeking new land and riches came in large ships. Their journeys across the Atlantic Ocean would take months, with the crew residing in tight quarters.

Ponce de León & the Everglades

Before the Europeans made it to Florida, the Calusa had heard what was happening — maybe first from their closest trading partners, the peaceful Taíno people of Cuba (then known as Hispaniola). They told stories of the Spaniards burning them to death and letting dogs tear them to pieces if they dared to fight back. So, when the Calusa saw the first European ship approach their shore in 1513, they were ready to protect themselves at all costs.

That first ship belonged to Spaniard Juan Ponce de León, and he most certainly meant them harm. A while back, León had enslaved the people of Puerto Rico. The Calusa probably did not know exactly who León was, but they had an idea of what he was up to. They did not let him stay long. Calusa warriors in canoes attacked his ship and drove León away.

León returned in 1521, with the hopes of building a settlement on the edge of the Everglades. This time he brought two ships full of men and supplies, and began ferrying them onto the beach.

The Calusa watched and waited. Once most of León's crew were stuck on shore, they launched their attack.

Spears and arrows tipped with pointed bone and fish spines whizzed out from behind the trees. They were sharp enough to pierce armor, and the Calusa also wielded shark-tooth war clubs. The Spanish stood no chance. Many were killed. León himself took a point to his thigh. Though he managed to flee to Cuba with a few survivors, he soon died from his wounds.

A Chance for Peace

After León's death, the Everglades continued on as it had for the last five thousand years. The lives of the birds, plants, bugs, trees, and alligators remained unchanged. But life started to change for the Calusa.

The Europeans continued their conquest across the Americas and the Spanish began to establish themselves farther north in the Tampa Bay area, and farther south in Miami. Disease and warfare

Spanish Weapons & Armor

Calusa Weapons

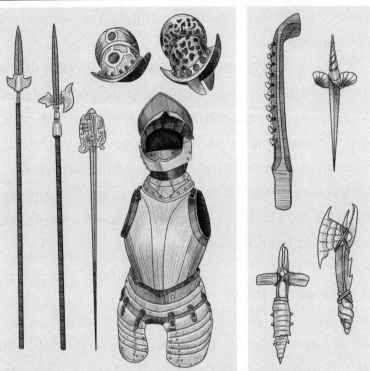

While the Spanish used weapons and armor made of steel, the Calusa had no armor and made weapons from shells, shark teeth, and other natural materials.

spread, and Indigenous people were captured and enslaved.

The leader of the Calusa, King Caalus, was young when his people first fought Ponce de León. But when he reached his sixties, he handed the crown to his 23-year-old son, also named Caalus. While the old king had vowed to keep colonizers away at any cost, now, with Spanish settlements in other parts of the Florida peninsula, it was up to his son to try to make peace.

So, in 1566, the young King Caalus (or Carlos, as the Europeans called him) invited the Spanish governor of Florida, Pedro Menéndez de Avilés, to a feast. Being mistrustful of each other, both leaders sought to demonstrate their power. Menéndez showed up with peculiar fanfare — 200 men, mostly soldiers, plus drummers, flag-bearers, trumpeters, a guitar, and a "dancing dwarf."

Caalus brought forth an elaborate meal of oysters, roasted fish, and hardtack biscuits. It was one of the first feasts in history shared by Native Americans and European settlers. The famous first Thanksgiving at Plymouth, Massachusetts, was still fifty-five years in the future.

The feast took place in Caalus' royal house. The structure was built on top of a man-made shell mound, overlooking the water. It stood on wooden stilts, with a thatched palm-frond roof. The Spanish found it impressive, especially since it was large enough to hold 2,000 people. That evening, King Caalus and Avilés agreed to peace.

A year or so later, the peace ended when Menéndez assassinated Caalus and his successor, Felipe. In the fighting that followed, the Calusa are said to have torched their own royal house in order to force the Europeans out of the area. It worked, and the Calusa were then able to keep the Spanish at bay for another two hundred years.

Though they remained free, the Everglades tribes began to decline because of European colonization farther north. Many were captured in slave raids. Some migrated to Cuba. An estimated ninety percent died from smallpox, yellow fever, and other European diseases. Those who lived closer to the Everglades and its marshes were better protected. They would soon be joined by others moving into the area. Collectively, they eventually all became known as the Seminoles and Miccosukees we know today.

Clues about the Calusa

What we know about the Calusa people comes from two sources: what the Europeans wrote about them, which is not always accurate, and the artifacts they left behind. Some of the biggest clues archaeologists find today are shell mounds, or middens. These are basically garbage heaps — and garbage is pretty interesting when it's a thousand years old.

Sometimes archaeologists find pottery and carved jewelry in the middens. But most of what's inside are shells from oysters, clams, conchs, and other shellfish. Some were thrown away after the animal inside was eaten. Others are the remains of broken tools.

Today, scientists find many artifacts along the coasts, where the towns were bigger. They also find some deep in the Everglades, in the hardwood hammock islands. In 2018 archaeologists made a particularly exciting find — part of King Caalus' royal home. It is on the top of Mound Key, near what we call Fort Myers Beach today.

CHAPTER FIVE

Seminoles, Gladesmen, & Greenbacks

THE EVERGLADES MEET THE INDUSTRIAL WORLD

In the 1700s, groups of Native Americans migrated south to Florida. They were trying to avoid conflicts up north with European settlers and other tribes, as hunting grounds fell to cotton plantations, farms, and cattle fields. Many were from the Creek cultures of Georgia and Alabama, including Miccosukees, Muscogees, Yamasees, Yuchis, Choctaws, Apalachees, Apalachicolas, Oconees, and Hitichis. Though they came from many nations, most white settlers did not make an effort to tell them apart. They called them all Seminoles.

It must have been heartbreaking to leave their homelands. Their ancestors had lived there for at least 12,000 years. But the Seminoles and Miccosukees soon succeeded in Florida. They farmed, raised livestock, traded with Europeans, and kept their hunting traditions alive. They accepted many into their society, joining with the remaining Calusa, Tequesta, and other Florida tribes.

They also protected Africans and African Americans who escaped slavery on plantations, welcoming them as free people. Many of them became known as Black Seminoles. Though they came from different continents, the Seminoles, Miccosukees, and Africans often had much in common. They shared similar customs and the ideals of working the land together for the good of the community.

But more and more white settlers moved south into Florida. Before long, again they wanted the land the Seminoles and Miccosukees lived on. They demanded the U.S. government get rid of them.

The government agreed. President James Monroe, and later President Andrew Jackson, signed laws that broke existing treaties, and called for all Native Americans east of the Mississippi River to be "removed" to the west. They authorized soldiers to invade and attack the Native Americans. A half-century of wars began.

The Seminole Wars

One group of people wanting to kill another is one of the great tragedies and bewilderments of humankind. Just like Ponce de León, many white settlers were sick with greed and racism. They did not see Native Americans as people or neighbors. They only saw profits. Profits from how they could use the land and sell into slavery the African Americans who lived with the Seminoles, plus some of the Seminoles and Miccosukees themselves.

It was a tragic time in history but one from which we can learn powerful lessons. We must realize when our actions are hurting others, and know that each one of us has the power to value kindness and other people's rights before money.

Most of the fighting took place north of the Everglades. Through each war, the Seminoles and Miccosukees fought fiercely for their land and freedom. They won many battles. There is not room in this book to tell the tales of the brave Seminole and Miccosukee warriors and leaders, like Osceola, Micanopy, Coacoochee (Wild Cat), Abika (Sam

Florida State Parks host reenactments of historical Florida events, including the Seminole Wars. The reenactors work to teach visitors about Florida's rich, and sometimes troubled, history.

Jones), and Halpuda Micco (Billy Bowlegs). But those are stories worth seeking out.

U.S. soldiers also fought boldly. Perhaps they battled for what they believed in, or maybe they did it because it was their job. They, too, won many battles. But as in all wars, everyone lost. Thousands of Seminoles, Miccosukees, Africans, African-Americans, U.S. soldiers, and others died, most in horrible ways. Soldiers chose to kill women and children and burn villages. People in government made new laws to make these tragedies legal.

After many years of fighting, white settlers forced most of the Seminoles and Miccosukees out of Florida and onto reservations in Oklahoma and Arkansas. They kidnapped many Black Seminoles — even those who were born free and whose ancestors had lived with the Seminoles for generations — and forced them to work as slaves on plantations.

Freedom in the Everglades

Meanwhile, the Everglades remained peaceful. Spoonbills waded in salt marshes, their pink feathers reflecting off of the still water. Caterpillars formed chrysalises and emerged as delicate yellow, blue, and orange butterflies. Young, pudgy manatee calves swam slowly through mangrove channels.

With each war, the remaining Seminoles and Miccosukees were pushed farther and farther south, until they ended up in the Everglades. It is here that the wars finally ended.

The sharp sawgrass, tropical hammocks, twisted mangroves, and cypress swamps protected

One way the Miccosukee and Seminole people adapted to living in the Everglades was by creating chickees, which are open-walled houses built from cypress logs, with palm-thatched roofs.

those who were left. Armies tried to breach the marsh, but mostly those men did not have the skills to navigate or survive in such a wilderness. So eventually, they gave up. Despite its best efforts, the U.S. government never got either tribe to surrender. Today, the Seminole are known as "the unconquered," as they never signed a peace treaty.

The Seminole and Miccosukee people still call the Everglades home, though their lives there have not always been easy. The government might have finally stopped the violence, but surviving in the marsh was difficult. The growing pressures of industrial development made it harder and harder to live off the land. For the next hundred years, many lived in poverty.

Today the Seminole Tribe of Florida remains closely connected to their ways and traditions, but are also successful in the modern economy. They own the Hard Rock Hotel & Casinos, which operates in seventy-four countries, along with one of the largest cattle operations in the U.S. Most today lead modern lives, while continuing to protect their culture and the land that guarded them. Some even earn their living sharing the nature of the Everglades and their traditions of sewing, patchwork, chickee building and alligator wrestling (which was once for hunting, but is now done for sport and entertainment) with visitors who have the desire to explore and learn.

The Gladesmen

After the Seminole Wars ended in 1858, a few white settlers began moving into the Everglades. But it was a hot, soggy place, full of mosquitoes and strange noises. There were no roads and traveling by boat was difficult. Alligators and venomous snakes seemed to lurk around every corner.

The Everglades were a wild frontier where only the toughest, most adventurous, or most desperate people dared travel. It was here that outlaws and bank robbers hid from the law, and bootleggers ran secret alcohol stills.

The early settlers had to learn how to live off the land. They traded with the Seminoles and Miccosukees, who in turn, shared their culture. These Gladesmen, as they began to be known, developed boats capable of navigating the marshes. They hunted and fished for their food. Today, some of their descendants still live in the Everglades. They share their ancestors' culture of independent spirit and knowledge of local nature.

One of the early Gladesmen was George Washington Storter, Jr. In the 1880s he farmed sugarcane and started a trading post that later became Everglades City. His store was one of the first places Seminoles traded with white settlers.

Historically, Gladesmen built small homes in the Everglades and lived off the land and water. Today, they live more modern lives, but are known for their keen awareness of nature and its treasures.

Eventually, towns developed on the outskirts of the marshes. Most were disorganized trading posts, but one was well planned. A yacht captain from Denmark, Peter Nelson, hoped to create a peaceful community. He named the town Alva, after the white flowers that grew on the river bank. In it he built churches, parks, and the Everglades' first school and library.

To navigate the waters and marshes of the Everglades, Gladesmen used a skiff, a small boat they pushed through the water with a long pole.

Way out on a lonely outpost island lived another interesting character. Juan Gomez was a Portuguese pirate who had survived a life of adventure. He claimed to have sailed with the infamous, yet fictional, pirate Gasparilla, spoke seven languages, and lived to be 119 years old. Legend has it, he buried treasure throughout the Everglades, which has yet to be found.

Though only a small number of people were hearty enough to live in the Everglades during this time, some changed the land for the worse. Hunters slaughtered millions of birds and land animals. They nearly caused the extinction of alligators, crocodiles, otters, foxes, panthers, bobcats, herons, ibis, spoonbills, and flamingos, just to name a few. Some they killed to sell as food; others for their hides and feathers, which were used to decorate fashionable ladies' hats. Some they just shot for entertainment. Sadly, hunting was only the beginning of the damage humans did to the Everglades.

Progress, Developers, & Politicians

Life inside the Everglades was isolated, but just outside, society began to bustle. Cities sprang up along the coasts. Miami, Fort Myers, and Coral Gables bounced to life. Soon, people clearcut the pine rocklands and cypress domes. The pinelands were ideal for humans to build upon, being dryer than the surrounding wetlands. People also needed wood for houses and ships, railroads and factories. They desired cleared land for grazing cattle and growing crops. Progress depended upon it.

Progress — it's usually those who work as real estate developers and politicians who like to misuse the word progress. Over thousands of years, geologic progress created one of the world's most important wetlands. Evolutionary progress led to wide-eyed green herons perched atop cypress knees and lizards whose skin perfectly matches tree bark.

But when people of little imagination looked out across the sparkling Everglades, all they saw was a waste of space. They envisioned a future land of shopping malls, vacation resorts, gas stations, and sugarcane mills. To them, profits from a parking lot were more intriguing than a pod of newborn alligators swimming between purple-flowered lily pads. The twisted, thousands-year-old cypress trees were no match for their kind of progress.

"Drain the swamp!" they yelled from their meeting rooms and podiums. "Reclamation" they called it. That word somehow suggested they would be rescuing the Everglades from what nature had done to it. Scientists tried to warn them of the damage they would cause, but their voices were too soft to be heard over the buzz of economic growth.

So, the workers dammed up Lake Okeechobee to stop the water from flowing into the marshes. Dynamite rang through the air as it blew apart ancient limestone. Fleets of dredges and bulldozers chugged black smoke as they dug canals and built levees to drain the land. It was a difficult and complicated task, but they were determined. They

Many Florida residents work to protect the environment from man-made dangers and threats. One is fracking, a method of extracting oil and gas from the earth.

touted man reshaping nature as a great feat of engineering — and the more land they dried out, the more money they made.

The Dying Marsh

Time went on. Cities glistened with skyscrapers, golf courses, swimming pools, and night clubs. In the country, farmers grew tomatoes, potatoes, and sugarcane. Semi-trucks drove their crops to grocery stores across the country. People were prospering, but the Everglades were dying.

House by house, construction workers paved over pinelands and sawgrass. Waste from factories crept into the heart of the swamps. Fertilizers and pesticides from farms poisoned the fish, insects, and gooey periphyton blobs, and created harmful algae blooms. Resort hotels covered up the sand-dune beaches where the Calusa once danced by the fire.

Most people did not notice. They were looking inward, toward the cities and their own busy lives. But a few looked outward, across the Everglades. And they were determined to save it.

CHAPTER SIX

Low Blows, High Hopes, & Heroes

SAVING THE EVERGLADES, THEN & NOW

A century ago, the Everglades' fate was bleak. Marshes were rapidly becoming farms and neighborhoods. Herons, otters, and panthers were nearly extinct. Even orchids were disappearing, as collectors stripped them from their tropical nests.

For those who wanted to protect the Everglades, convincing the public was no easy task. That's because most people thought of it as a dismal swamp, if they even thought about it at all. It was not enough to love the land, water, and creatures. To make positive change, the Everglades heroes had to use science and education.

Biologists, geologists, ecologists, and naturalists

studied the wilderness. Their research proved the wetlands were vital to the well-being of Florida, and of the world. Journalists, teachers, poets, socialites, activists, politicians, and volunteers worked to change perceptions. People started to pay attention. Eventually, many recognized the Everglades for what it is — one of the world's natural treasures.

Bird conservation groups, like the Audubon Society, led the way. In 1902, they hired the

Everglades' first game warden, Guy Bradley. His job was to stop people from killing herons, egrets, and other birds illegally for their feathers. A few years later, in 1905, he was murdered by a father hunting with his two sons. His death inspired

The National Fish and Wildlife Foundation established an award to honor Guy Bradley in 1988. The award recognizes individuals for achievements in wildlife law enforcement.

politicians to pass laws to help birds. In 2023 they renamed the Guy Bradley Visitor Center in his honor.

The Miccosukee and Seminole people have also done much for the Everglades. One seldom-heard story is how they saved the deer. Ranchers believed deer were spreading disease to their cattle (though there was no science to prove it), so they ordered deer herds in south Florida to be killed. After some time, the only remaining deer, about 400, were on the reservations. The tribes refused to allow access. Later, scientists proved that the deer were not actually a threat, and the hunts were called off.

Other early guardians of the Everglades include: Mary Mann Jennings, who helped create Royal Palm State Park, which is now part of Everglades

Minnie Moore-Willson was an advocate for the Seminole people. She supported the conservation of their culture and fought for the Everglades to be seen as their rightful home.

National Park; Minnie Moore-Willson, who was a writer and Native American rights advocate, and helped create bird sanctuaries; and botanist John K. Small, who researched and documented many plants and animals in southern Florida.

Everglades National Park

It took many people to help save the Everglades, but it was especially the passion of one man that turned it into a national park. Ernest F. Coe, or Tom, as his friends called him, didn't meet the Everglades until he was sixty years old. But when he and his wife, Anna, moved to Florida in 1925, he fell in love with the landscape. He spent hours walking through, and even sleeping out in, the wilderness. No mosquitoes, snakes, or poisonous plants could keep him from admiring what he called a "great empire of solitude."

It took six years from the time Tom proposed the park until President Franklin D. Roosevelt approved it. After another thirteen years, it officially opened in 1947. If you visit today, you might just end up in the

Ernest F. Coe Visitor Center named in Tom's honor.

That same year, a book came out that caused many more to care about the marsh. While writing *The Everglades: River of Grass*, Marjory Stoneman Douglas fell in love with the Everglades. She ended up devoting the rest of her life to protecting the land, waters, and their wild inhabitants — and hers was a long life. She died in 1998 at age 108. Her book is still considered one of the most important nature writings of all time, and today most people still use her phrase, "river of grass," when describing the Everglades.

Marjory Stoneman Douglas was an Everglades advocate. She is known as the "Mother of the Everglades," and her environmental group, Friends of the Everglades, still works to preserve the land and waters today.

It Takes a Nation

Becoming a national park was a great start, but many threats to the Everglades happen outside of its boundaries. Thanks to the writings of Douglas and others, like Rachel Carson, people in the U.S. government also passed acts to protect endangered species and clean air and water. They banned pesticides, like DDT, in 1972 and poisons, like leaded gasoline, in the 1980s.

Gradually, the Everglades and many other lands and waters across the country began to heal. Species that were nearly extinct rebounded, like osprey,

In 1966, President Lyndon B. Johnson signed the Clean Waters Restoration Act in an effort to reduce water pollution.

pelicans, manatees, and alligators. Not all animals were so lucky, though. Ivory-billed woodpeckers and Carolina parakeets will never be seen again.

People who usually don't agree with one another have also put aside their differences to save the Everglades. In the 1960s, conservationists and hunters successfully fought the construction of a jetport right outside of the park, which would have disrupted the wilds with noise and pollution.

This was a difficult accomplishment and a major win for the Everglades, and was the catalyst for Douglas to found the nonprofit Friends of the Everglades, which continues today. Joe Browder of the Audubon Society also helped greatly in stopping the jetport, by joining with Buffalo Tiger of the Miccosukee and getting the hunters on board, even though they didn't like the Audubon Society because it urged to them to stop killing alligators.

Then in the 1990s, the Florida legislature passed the Everglades Forever Act, to help clean pollutants from the water. A few years later, President Bill Clinton and Florida Governor Jeb Bush passed a budget act to further help Everglades restoration.

Young People Make a Difference

Also in the 1990s, a wealthy developer wanted to build a large theme park on the edge of the Everglades. Although it sounded like it might be a fun place to visit, with rides, virtual reality games, and movies, it would have hurt the Everglades with noise, pollution, and destruction of wetlands. Many young people spoke up. They said the Everglades were more important than a tourist attraction — and people listened. The park was never built.

The kids, who were fourth and fifth graders, went on to create a conservation and education organization with help from their teachers, Connie Washburn and Marta Whitehouse. Young Friends of the Everglades began with Douglas' blessing, and some of the students even met her in person. Today, new students continue to join the Young Friends (or Marjory's Echo, as they sometimes call themselves). They plant trees, explore the marshes, go to rallies, and speak their minds to politicians — and you're welcome to join them!

Today's Dangers

Still today, even with all that we now know, the Everglades are in danger. The reasons are mostly the same as they were a century ago.

Water quantity: Dams and canals stop water from flowing naturally, which creates problems for plants and animals that have evolved to benefit from its natural wet and dry seasons. It's also especially damaging to sea life. In 2015, twenty percent of the seagrass in the Florida Bay died because people diverted too much fresh water away from it, which made the salt content (salinity) too high.

Water quality: Many unhealthy ingredients enter the Everglades from upstream. Pesticides poison some plants and animals. Fertilizers and human waste encourage algae blooms (sometimes called toxic green tides), and invasive plants like cattails displace sawgrass. Fertilizer pollution also worsens red tides along the coasts, which are particularly deadly to ocean wildlife. In Florida Bay, pollutants are killing seagrass and the shellfish,

fish, sponges, and other creatures who depend on that habitat. Further out, poor water quality from the Everglades is harming the Keys' barrier reef, causing coral bleaching and contributing to disease and the death of the reefs. All of this also hurts the many people and communities who depend on tourism and fishing for their incomes.

To make matters worse, the rain sometimes contains mercury, which likely enters the air from factories around the planet. Sulfates (which come primarily from the many sugarcane farms) combine with mercury to form the deadly compound methylmercury. Microorganisms absorb the methylmercury and it accumulates farther up the food chain to toxic levels. As a result, some fish in the Everglades are now unsafe for humans to eat more than once in a while.

Habitat destruction: Houses, farms, and ranches continue replacing wetlands. Only about half of the original Everglades ecosystem remains, and more is lost every day. Some habitats, like custard-apple forests, are gone for good. Others are in significant danger of disappearing. In 2017 a developer clear-cut some of the last unprotected pine rocklands in order to build a shopping center and some restaurants. A year later, an oil company destroyed old-growth trees in Big Cypress National Preserve, looking for places to drill and frack.

Population: Of course, as long as the human population continues to grow, new apartments and roads must be built somewhere, and that is almost always on lands that were once wild. In the last century, more than ninety percent of wading birds have disappeared from the Everglades. In the next twenty years, the human population of south Florida is expected to grow by almost 300 percent, from eight million to twenty million, and that doesn't even include tourists.

More cars on the roads are also particularly dangerous for Florida panthers. Each year twenty or more are killed by cars.

Invasive species: There are dozens of plants and animal species that are threatening native species. For example, people brought melaleuca trees from

In 1995 the Florida panther was near extinction with only twenty-five left in the wild. Thanks to conservation efforts, there are now around two hundred.

Australia a century ago to try to dry up the Everglades to make it suitable for farming and building houses. Today those, along with invasive Brazilian pepper trees, continue to overtake sawgrass habitats and the homes of the wildlife who live there. Burmese pythons, from people releasing their unwanted pets, have now eaten more than ninety percent of the mammals in the Everglades, including opossums, raccoons, and rabbits.

Climate change and sea level rise: In a place where most of the land is only a foot or two above sea level, rising oceans pose many problems. One is salt water overtaking freshwater marshes (saltwater intrusion). This threatens the balance of the ecosystem and the aquifer on which millions of people depend for daily water. Also, seagrass and sawgrass habitats are very effective carbon sinks (habitats that remove carbon from the atmosphere and store it indefinitely). As they are further damaged and destroyed, they release greenhouse gases into the atmosphere, making global warming worse. Other climate change threats come from changing weather patterns, like unpredictable rainfall, warming ocean waters, and more intense hurricanes.

Greed and corruption: Scientists believe many of these problems are solvable with enough time, money, and cooperation. But like a century ago, greed often prevents people from doing the right thing for the environment and future generations. A major challenge with helping the Everglades today comes from real estate development, sugarcane farming, ranching, and other agricultural-based industries, which donate to politicians who then pass laws to allow their businesses to act irresponsibly toward the land and the planet.

Looking Forward

The problems facing the Everglades and our planet are upsetting to think about. Because of our ignorance and short-sightedness as humans, there are cultures, species, and landscapes that will never exist again. And though we cannot erase the harm our ancestors have done, we can most certainly learn from their mistakes in order to change things for the better in the future.

It is important to remember that it was individuals who caused these problems. Some knew they were doing harm. Some did not. But as individuals, each of us has the power and responsibility to educate ourselves about how to make the world a more peaceful place — for humans, herons, pinelands, dragonflies, periphyton blobs, and all things in between.

As before, to make positive change it is not enough to just love the land, water, and creatures. The next generation of Everglades heroes will also need to use science and education. Through science we can reduce the causes of global warming, especially lessening our reliance on fossil fuels, and creating less harmful methods of farming.

Through education, we can shift our thinking from seeing the land as something that exists for our profits (a commodity), to understanding that we are just one small part of a complex ecological community — a community on which our survival as a species depends.

Many volunteers and organizations work to help keep Florida waters and beaches clean, plus educate people about nature. They can always use an extra hand, if you want to get involved!

And in the meantime, at least for a while, the Everglades still offer a vast and peaceful solitude. Sitting in a field of sawgrass, it's easy to imagine everything that came before. The mammoths trumpet. The Calusa people paddle in dugout canoes. The vultures quietly ride the updrafts. Storm clouds darken the skies. Lightning cracks. And the rains, once again, flood the great marsh.

A World Wonder

The Everglades are not just important to the United States. People around the world have recognized it as a special place. It currently holds the titles of International Biosphere Reserve, Wetland of International Importance, and World Heritage Site.

CHAPTER SEVEN

Adventure Trails & Alligator Tails

MINI-GUIDE TO VISITING THE EVERGLADES

Everglades National Park is special. Instead of preserving dramatic geology like mountains and canyons, or human history like battlefields and forts, Everglades National Park is all about its diversity of life. That means visiting the park is a one-of-a-kind adventure that requires getting out of the car and into the wilderness.

Seasons

What to do depends partly on the time of year you visit. Most people like to visit in the winter, between December and April. This is the dry season, which makes hiking and biking easier. Birds are plentiful and rainstorms are less likely. But the real reason most people visit in the winter is because it's more comfortable. The weather is cooler and the mosquitoes are less pesky.

Summers are also a fascinating time in the Everglades. In the wet season, afternoon thunderheads build up high and fast, like giant

The Everglades only experience two seasons: a wet season and a dry one. The wet season is from mid-May through November and is the time when most rain storms occur. The dry season goes from December into May. Animals have adapted to survive during these distinct weather changes.

cauliflowers heads over the sawgrass. Insects, fish, and frogs come to life in the water. Trails are not crowded, but the air is hot and humid and not entirely comfortable.

In the spring and fall, thousands of birds pause here to rest and refuel during their migrations north and south respectively. Some stop just for an hour or two, others for weeks. Warblers, vultures, and hummingbirds are just a few of the usual suspects.

Things to Do (Inside & Outside of the Park)

Hike: While the Everglades are vast, it only takes a short walk to see most of its habitats. The Pineland Trail is just 0.4 miles and has a wheelchair-accessible dirt path through palmettos and pines. The Anhinga Trail winds atop a boardwalk through the sawgrass marsh. It's full of wildlife, including birds, alligators, and turtles. To see the hardwood hammock, try the Mahogany Trail, which ends up at the biggest mahogany tree in the country.

Slough Slog: For a real adventure, follow a ranger on a slough slog. Bushwhack through grass and into dark cypress domes. Wear long pants and shoes you don't mind getting wet, and make reservations.

Bicycle: There are five trails in the Everglades National Park that can take you through the pinelands, hammocks, and prairies.

Tram: For a lazier day, try a two-hour tram ride through Shark Valley, where a naturalist will tell you about the alligators and birds, including the endangered Everglade snail kite and its main food source, giant apple snails.

Airboats and Swamp Buggies: Zooming through the marsh is as exciting as any rollercoaster. Gladesmen

Everglades bike trails include: Shark Valley Tram Road, Snake Bight Trail, Rowdy Bend Trail, Long Pine Key Nature Trail, and the L-67 Canal Road.

and members of the Seminole and Miccosukee tribes all offer tours. Some also have wildlife parks, where you can get up close with alligators, snakes, and other charming creatures.

Kayak & Canoe: Expert paddlers should try the ninety-nine-mile Wilderness Waterway Trail. But most people prefer just an hour or two floating along mangrove-lined rivers with manatees and dolphins. Rent boats or find a guided tour at the Flamingo and Gulf Coast visitor centers.

Ah-Tah-Thi-Ki Museum: Learn about Seminole culture, past and present, on the Big Cypress Indian Reservation. Plan extra time to watch the film and walk the boardwalk trail.

Airboats, also called fan boats, are powered by a large, above-water propeller that glides the boat across the water's surface. They have a flat bottom that allows them to easily travel through shallow waters without getting stuck.

Miccosukee Indian Village: Miccosukee culture comes to life here, with beadwork and basket weaving. Of course, there are also alligators, plus airboat rides to a hammock-style camp.

Museums: Good places to learn about the Gladesmen and other pioneer families of the Everglades are the Museum of the Everglades in Everglades City; the Smallwood Store just down the road in Chokoloskee; and the Collier County Museums in Naples, Immokalee, and Marco Island.

Motorboat: If you're not up for paddling, hop aboard a gas-powered boat to explore the islands in the bay with a tour-guide captain.

Missile Silo: Learn about the Cold War and see relics, including a missile inside the abandoned Nike Hercules base. Reservations are needed for a tour.

Eat: The Everglades have some specific cuisine. Try Seminole sofkee (similar to porridge) and fry bread. Or for brave stomachs, there's 'gator-tail sausage, jerky, and fried bites.

In 1953, an old shed was converted into the world's smallest post office. The building is 61.3 square feet and located near the national park in Ochopee, Florida.

Become a Ranger...

...Or at least hang out with one for a while. The rangers at Everglades National Park love to show off nature to kids and talk about spoonbills, sawgrass, periphyton blobs, and Calusa warriors. Join them for a hike, bike ride, or kayak trip. With a little work, you can also become an Everglades National Park Junior Ranger. To get started, grab a book at any visitor center.

Visitor Centers

Since the park is so big — 1.5 million acres — it's smart to think about where you want to go before you get there. There are three main entrances and four visitor centers to start the day, where you can ask for advice from rangers, explore nature exhibits, and get your National Parks Passport stamped.

Gulf Coast: This is the closest entrance to Naples (45-minute drive) and the west coast of Florida. It's all about boating here, since it's a gateway to Florida Bay and the mangroves of Ten Thousand Islands. It's the smallest visitor center, but it's right in Everglades City, which has a few restaurants, boat tours, and kayak rentals.

Shark Valley: Between Naples (80 minutes) and Miami (50 minutes), this is the place to hop on the tram or rent bicycles. There are snacks here, too.

Ernest F. Coe: This large visitor center also has educational films and local art displays. Learn about hurricanes, too, including Irma, a Category 4 storm that

Park rangers are a vital part of the Everglades experience. They educate, lead, and protect the land and its visitors.

hit the park in 2017. The visitor center is 20 minutes from Homestead and an hour from Miami.

Royal Palm: Visit this center and join a guided tour of the Anhinga or Gumbo Limbo Trails. It's just a few minutes past the Coe center. This center has two wheelchair accessible trails as well.

Guy Bradley Visitor Center at Flamingo: At the end of the land (an hour from Homestead), Flamingo is for hiking, boating, and watching the sunset. There are also displays, boat tours, rentals for kayaks, canoes, and bikes, and the Flamingo Lodge & Restaurant.

Big Cypress National Preserve: Just north of Everglades National Park, this vast, swampy wilderness between Naples and Miami is part of the Everglades ecosystem. Stop at either of its visitor centers for exhibits, films, ranger tours, and a stroll down a boardwalk with alligator-viewing areas. Rangers here can also show you where to go for a scenic drive, hike, or bicycle ride.

Tamiami Trail: U.S. Highway 41, a.k.a. Old Alligator Alley, crosses the state through the Everglades. Even

Visitors can see the Everglades from new heights atop the Shark Valley Observation Tower. The structure is seventy feet tall, giving people a view as far as twenty miles.

if you're not stopping to explore on this trip, you can still keep an eye out for wildlife along this road, including designated alligator-viewing sites. You might also notice that part of this road has been turned into bridges, which are now allowing more water to flow into the sloughs to help revive habitats.

Camping and Hotels

The only hotel in the park is the Flamingo Lodge at the southern end of the park. Otherwise, it's all about camping here. Flamingo has glamping tents and campgrounds with showers, restrooms, and grills. Primitive campsites are scattered through the rest of the park and on some beaches. Some you need a boat to get to, like elevated chickee platforms in the bay and on some other waterways.

Everglades City and Chokoloskee both have cabin rentals and a hotel or two. There are a couple of chickees for rent near Ochopee. Otherwise, most people stay in Marco Island and Naples to the west, and Homestead, Florida City, and Miami to the east.

Safety & What to Bring

Even in the winter, it will likely be warm and sunny. Pack a hat, sunglasses, sunscreen, and bug spray. Long pants, sleeves, and shoes (not sandals) are a good idea for hiking and to keep biting bugs and

In January 2019, Everglades City was designated a "Florida Trail Town" by Florida's Office of Greenways and Trails. This is because of the city's many miles of hiking, paddling, and biking trails.

sunburns away. Bring lots of water and snacks in the car and in your pack.

There are plants and animals in the Everglades that can hurt you, but they probably won't, as long as you use a little common sense and care. Watch for

Chickees

Look for these traditional Seminole houses, made from cypress logs and palm-thatch roofs. Their ancestors developed them during the Seminole Wars, when they had to be able to break camp quickly to escape U.S. soldiers. Today, most Seminoles live in regular houses, but chickee-style structures are a favorite with restaurants and roadside fruit stands.

snakes and alligators when walking. Give all wildlife plenty of space. Never get near an alligator, even if it looks like it is sleeping. Keep an eye out for poisonwood trees and poison ivy along the road and trails. Stop at a visitor center to find out what those plants look like, and for more safety advice.

It's also important to keep the creatures safe from you. Never feed wildlife. Besides making them sick, it can make them become too accustomed to people, which can get them into a

The Skunk Ape is a legendary seven-foot-tall Sasquatch relative who roams the Everglades.

lot of trouble. Sometimes it can make them aggressive or encourage them to get too close to dangerous roadways. Also, getting too close to birds can cause them to abandon their nests, which can kill their chicks. If birds look like they are thinking about flying away, that means you are probably too close.

Other Wild Lands to Explore

The original Everglades ecosystem once reached all the way from Orlando to the Florida Bay. About half of it is gone now. Luckily many areas of the remaining wilderness are now protected. Parks formed to preserve Everglades and related ecosystems include:

- Everglades National Park
- Big Cypress National Preserve
- Corkscrew Swamp Sanctuary
- Florida Panther National Wildlife Refuge
- Loxahatchee National Wildlife Refuge
- Fakahatchee Strand State Park

- Collier Seminole State Park
- Everglades Headwater National Wildlife Refuge
- Biscayne National Park

Nearby in Dry Tortugas National Park, less than one percent of the park is land, so visitors snorkel and scuba dive to explore and learn about Florida's marine ecosystems.

"There are no other Everglades in the world. They are, they have always been, one of the unique regions of the earth; remote, never wholly known."
— *Marjory Stoneman Douglas, opening lines of "The Everglades: River of Grass"*

"My temple is the swamp... When I would recreate myself, I seek the darkest wood, the thickest and most impenetrable and to the citizen, most dismal, swamp. I enter a swamp as a sacred place... I seemed to have reached a new world, so wild a place...far away from human society."
— *Henry David Thoreau, in his book "Walden and Other Writings"*

"We abuse land because we regard it as a commodity belonging to us. When we see land as a community to which we belong, we may begin to use it with love and respect."
— *Aldo Leopold, in his book "A Sand County Almanac"*

AUTHOR BIO

Karuna Eberl has lived and worked in the Florida Keys, writing for local and national publications, with an emphasis on nature, sustainability, history, and diversity. She has won multiple awards for her nature writing from the Outdoor Writers Association of America, the Society of American Travel Writers, and the Florida Outdoor Writers Association. Her credits include the BBC, National Parks Conservation Association, Atlas Obscura, Readers Digest, Family Handyman, Keys Weekly, FloridaRambler. com, and others. She has co-authored two editions of the award-winning Quixotic Key West & the Lower Keys Travel Guide. She has also produced a dozen indie films, produced and written for TV series on networks including National Geographic and the Discovery Channel, and directed the award-winning documentary *The Guerrero Project*, about the search for a sunken slave ship in the Florida Keys.

Acidification: ocean water absorbing excess carbon dioxide, which harms and kills corals and shelled marine life

Aestivate: when an animal becomes dormant during dry or hot seasons

Algae bloom: sudden growth of toxic algae, can be caused by phosphorous in fertilizer runoff or sewage

Amphibians: cold-blooded vertebrates with skin, like salamanders, frogs, and toads

Aquifer: groundwater stored within porous or permeable rock, used for drinking water

Archaeologist: a person who studies human life through artifacts left behind

Brackish: water with more salt than freshwater, but less salt than seawater, found in estuaries

Calcium carbonate: the chemical compound of limestone and the shells of marine organisms

Camouflage: physically matching its environment, such as an insect blending into its environment to avoid predators

Conquistador: a soldier or conqueror from Spain and Portugal, from the 1400s to the 1600s

Conservationist: a person who strives to protect plants, animals, and their habitats

Crustaceans: usually aquatic animals with an exoskeleton, like lobsters, shrimp, crabs, and barnacles

Cycad: an ancient family of plant, to which coontie (arrowroot) belongs

Cypress: a type of conifer tree that can grow in water; they live long and grow slowly

Cypress knees: woody knobs that grow up from a cypress tree's roots, especially when they're submerged in water

Ecologist: a person who studies how plants and animals interact in their ecosystem

Ecosystem: a community of plants, animals, and their surroundings, like water, air, and soil

Endangered: an animal or plant that is in danger of becoming extinct

Epiphytes: plants that grow on the surface of another plant, like air plants and some orchids

Estuary: a body of water where freshwater from a river meets ocean waters; a habitat for animals who can tolerate brackish water

Fracking: a method to extract oil and gas from rock

Glamping: glamorous camping, or luxury camping, in tents, yurts, and other structures

Habitats: types of natural environments, where plants and animals live, like beaches or forests

Hardwood hammock: a shady habitat with dry land and tropical/subtropical trees

Herbivores: organisms that feed mostly on plants, like marsh rabbits and white-tailed deer

Ignorance: having a lack of knowledge, information, or understanding about something

Invasive species: plants or animals not native to an ecosystem, which can cause harm

Invertebrates: animals without a backbone, including insects, crabs, and squid

Karst: limestone that's been weathered and partly dissolved, and is now jagged, often with sinkholes, spires and other rock formations

Levee: a man-made embankment, wall, or dam designed to prevent flooding

Limestone: a sedimentary rock often made from the skeletons of tiny marine life and coral

Mammals: warm-blooded vertebrates that nurse their young, like humans, bats, and whales

Mangroves: tropical trees with tangled roots that can tolerate salt water

Marsh: a wetland dominated mostly by grass, sedges, or reeds

Midden (or kitchen midden): an ancient human garbage dump, often containing shells, animal bones, and tools

Mollusks: aquatic animals with shells, like oysters and snails, and sometimes without, like octopuses

Morse Code: a system of communication using combinations of short and long tones to represent letters, used on the telegraph and by the military

Naturalist: a person who is interested in plants and animals in their natural surroundings

Ooids: small spheres that form when sand or other particles get coated with precipitated minerals (often calcium carbonate) as they roll back and forth in shallow-water

Palm: a tree with fan-shaped leaves (but scientifically more closely related to grass than trees)

Palmettos: palm plants with fan-shaped leaves, often the size of a bush

Peat: a dark, boggy soil made of partially decomposed plants

Peninsula: a piece of land that is mostly surrounded by water

Periphyton: colonies of algae, bacteria, and tiny freshwater animals

Pesticides: chemicals used for killing unwanted plants, insects, and other animals

Pine rockland: a habitat with dry, hard, rocky ground, pine trees, and shrubby palms

Pleistocene Epoch: a period in geological time from about 2.58 million to 11,700 years ago, which included the most recent Ice Age

Prairie: a mostly tree-less landscape and habitat, with grass and sedges

Precipitated: when a mineral, like calcium carbonate, is no longer dissolved in water, and instead becomes a solid, like limestone

Reptiles: cold-blooded vertebrates with scales, like turtles, snakes, lizards, and alligators

Salinity: the amount of salt dissolved in a water habitat

Sawgrass: a tall sedge (grass-like plant) with sharp edges

Sedges: grass-like plants, with solid stems and triangular edges (vs. grasses, which have hollow stems and are round or flat)

Sediment: layers of organic matter or minerals

Shellfish: aquatic animals with a shell, including mollusks and crustaceans

Slough: deeper river channel and habitat that stays wet all year, pronounced slew

Solidified: when a mineral like calcium carbonate is no longer suspended (dissolved) in water and becomes a solid

Spanish Moss: a native plant with wiry branching stems that often hangs from live oak trees in Florida

Swamp: a wetland dominated mostly by woody shrubs and trees

Vertebrates: animals that have vertebrae, meaning a backbone or a spine

Weathering: chemical or mechanical process where objects are changed by the forces of weather, like wind and water

Wetland: a habitat saturated with water, like a swamp, marsh, or bog

500 - 125,000 BCE

Porous Miami limestone layer deposited (basis of Biscayne Aquifer)

Last Ice Age, megafauna rules south Florida, first people probably arrive

Climate becomes sub-tropical, forming the Everglades

1500 - 1899

First known Calusa culture in South Florida (at least 2,000 years ago, though likely earlier)

1521 - Ponce de León becomes Calusa's first known contact with Europeans

1566 - Florida governor Menéndez de Avilés feasts with King Caalus

1569 - Avilés assassinates King Caalus

1760s - Most remaining Calusa and Tequesta move to Cuba

1835 - Second Seminole War begins, and lasts for seven years

1850 - First talks about draining the Everglades begin

1855 - Third Seminole War starts, mostly over land disputes

1890s - Seminoles and whites trade mostly peacefully in the Everglades

1896 - 50,000 acres of Everglades drained so far, sugarcane and rice crops popular

1900 - 1949

1902 - Guy Bradley becomes first game warden in Everglades, killed in 1905

1911 - Big Cypress Indian Reservation established

1920s - Real estate and farming booms as Everglades continue to be drained

1930 - Hoover Dike approved to dam Lake Okeechobee, after flooding deaths

1947 - Everglades officially becomes a national park

1948 - Another massive, 20-year draining project starts, led by Army Corps of Engineers

1950-1999

1957 - The Seminole Tribe of Florida is officially recognized by U.S. government

1962 - The Miccosukee Tribe of Indians of Florida is officially recognized by U.S. government

1968 - Conservationists and hunters successfully defeat proposed jet port in Big Cypress

1971 - Kissimmee River straightened by Army Corps, wetlands turned into cattle pastures

1972 - Clean Water Act passed by U.S. government

1974 - Big Cypress National Preserve established

1987 - First water cleanup plan for Everglades begins being developed

1990 - Sugarcane fields in northern Everglades are up to 450,000 acres

1992 - Hurricane Andrew, a Category 5 storm, heavily damages the Everglades

1994 - Florida passes Everglades Forever Act, to fix water quality, protect birds

1994 - Young Friends of the Everglades prevent theme park

2000-2024

2000 - Pres. Clinton, Gov. Bush sign Comprehensive Everglades Restoration Project

2000 - First confirmed breeding of invasive Burmese pythons in the Everglades

2015 - Drought raises salinity levels in Florida Bay, causing large seagrass die-off

2017 - Hurricane Irma heavily damages Everglades, Category 4 storm

1400s

1450 - Johannes Gutenberg invents movable-type printing press
1452 - Italian artist and inventor Leonardo da Vinci is born

1492 - Columbus firsts makes landfall in the Americas, in the Bahamas

1510 - Slave ship reaches south Florida, first known European contact with locals
1513 - Florida becomes Spanish territory

1519 - Magellan proves the earth is round by sailing around it
1500s
1521 - Spanish conquistadors conquer Cuba and the Aztecs in Mexico
1523 - Spanish conquistadors conquer the Incas in South America

1500s-1600s - European countries establish the slave trade in west Africa for labor for sugar, tobacco and cotton plantations

1600s
1600s - British and French settlements established in North America
1600s - Scientist Galileo Galilei proves that Earth orbits the sun

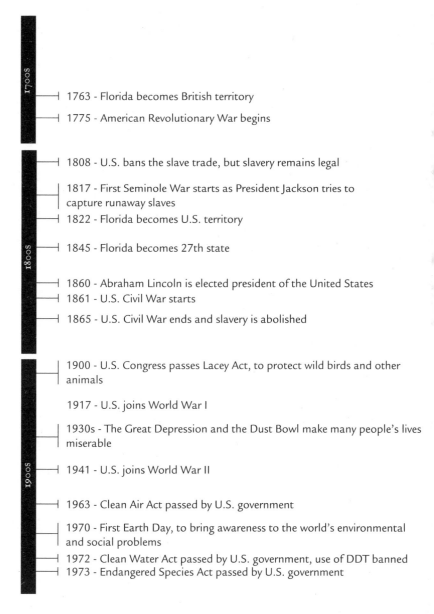

1700s

1763 - Florida becomes British territory

1775 - American Revolutionary War begins

1800s

1808 - U.S. bans the slave trade, but slavery remains legal

1817 - First Seminole War starts as President Jackson tries to capture runaway slaves

1822 - Florida becomes U.S. territory

1845 - Florida becomes 27th state

1860 - Abraham Lincoln is elected president of the United States

1861 - U.S. Civil War starts

1865 - U.S. Civil War ends and slavery is abolished

1900s

1900 - U.S. Congress passes Lacey Act, to protect wild birds and other animals

1917 - U.S. joins World War I

1930s - The Great Depression and the Dust Bowl make many people's lives miserable

1941 - U.S. joins World War II

1963 - Clean Air Act passed by U.S. government

1970 - First Earth Day, to bring awareness to the world's environmental and social problems

1972 - Clean Water Act passed by U.S. government, use of DDT banned

1973 - Endangered Species Act passed by U.S. government

REFERENCES

Douglas, Marjory Stonemen. 2016. *The Everglades: River of Grass*. Pineapple Press, Third Edition.

McCally, David. 2002. *The Everglades: An Environmental History*. University Press of Florida.

Lodge, Thomas W. 1994. *The Everglades Handbook*. CRC Press.

Grunwald, Michael. 2007. *The Swamp: The Everglades, Florida, and hte Politics of Paradise*. Simon & Schuster.

Mclver, Stuart B. 2009. *Death to the Everglades: The Murder of Guy Bradley, America's First Martyr to Environmentalism*. University Press of Florida.

FURTHER READING & VIDEOS

Alden, Peter & Cech, Rick. 1998. *National Audubon Society Field Guide to Florida*. Knopf. https://www.nps.gov/ever/learn/photosmultimedia/mountainsandvalleys.htm

Ake, Anne. 2017. *Everglades: An Ecosystem Facing Challenges and Choices*. Pineapple Press.

Douglas, Marjory Stoneman. 1986. *River of Grass*. R Bemis Pub Ltd.

George, Jean Craighead. 1997. *Everglades* Harper Collins.

George, Jean Craighead. 1997. *The Talking Earth* Harper Collins.

Lourie, Peter. 1994. *Evergladews: Buffalo Tiger and the River of Grass*. Highlights Press.

Lyncg, Wayne. 2007. *The Everglades* Cooper Square Publishing.

Raffa, Edwina & Rigsby, Annelle. 2006. *Escape the Everglades*. Pineapple Press.

Stone, Mac. 2014. *Everglades: America's Wetlands*. University of Florida.

INDEX

INDEX

All About... Series

A series for inquisitive young readers

If you liked this book, you may also enjoy:

Also available as an audiobook!

All titles are available in print and ebook form!
Teachers guides and puzzles available at brpressbooks.com/all-about-teachers-guides/